JOHN**PATITUCCI** WALKING BASS

How to Play Walking Basslines On Any Chord Sequence - For Upright & Electric Bass

JOHN**PATITUCCI**

With Tim Pettingale

FUNDAMENTAL**CHANGES**

John Patitucci Walking Bass

How to Play Walking Basslines On Any Chord Sequence - For Upright & Electric Bass

ISBN: 978-1-78933-213-1

Published by www.fundamental-changes.com

www.fundamental-changes.com

Over 13,000 fans on Facebook: **FundamentalChangesInGuitar**

Instagram: **FundamentalChanges**

For over 350 Free Guitar Lessons with Videos Check Out

www.fundamental-changes.com

Connect with John:

https://johnpatitucci.com

https://www.facebook.com/John-Patitucci-131251177024/

https://www.instagram.com/johnjpatitucci/

Cover Image Copyright: author photo used by permission

Special thanks to Ron Knights for audio mixing (http://ronknights.co.uk) and Johnny Cox/Luke Lewis for assistance with notation.

Contents

About the Author

John Patitucci began playing the electric bass at the age of 10 and was performing and composing music by the time he was 12. Aged 15 he began to play the acoustic bass and also took up the piano a year later. He quickly moved from playing soul and rock to blues, jazz and classical music, and his eclectic tastes caused him to explore all types of music as a player and composer.

As a studio musician, John has played on countless albums with artists such as B.B. King, Bonnie Raitt, Chick Corea, Wayne Shorter, Herbie Hancock, Michael Brecker, George Benson, Dizzy Gillespie, Was Not Was, Dave Grusin, Natalie Cole, Bon Jovi, Sting, Queen Latifah and Carly Simon.

As a performer, John has played throughout the world with his own band and with jazz luminaries Chick Corea, Herbie Hancock, Wayne Shorter, Stan Getz, Pat Metheny, Wynton Marsalis, Joshua Redman, Michael Brecker, McCoy Tyner, Nancy Wilson, Randy Brecker, Freddie Hubbard, Tony Williams, Hubert Laws, Hank Jones, Mulgrew Miller, James Williams, Kenny Werner and scores of others. Some of the many pop and Brazilian artists he has played with include Sting, Aaron Neville, Natalie Cole, Joni Mitchell, Carole King, Milton Nascimiento, Astrud and Joao Gilberto, Airto and Flora Purim, Ivan Lins, Joao Bosco and Dori Caymmi.

John's many recordings with Chick Corea's Elektric Band and Akoustic Band, and the Wayne Shorter Quartet, plus sixteen solo recordings have earned him four Grammy Awards (three for playing and one for composition) and over fifteen Grammy nominations. In addition, his first solo recording, *John Patitucci*, went to number one on the Billboard Jazz charts. His latest release in 2019 was a predominantly solo bass recording entitled *Soul of the Bass*, on Three Faces Records.

In 2000, John began touring again with the legendary Wayne Shorter. The Wayne Shorter Quartet, featuring Danilo Perez on piano and Brian Blade on drums, has received worldwide acclaim for its performances and recordings. Their live recording *Footprints Live* was nominated for a Grammy in 2001 and a studio recording, *Alegria*, won a Grammy in 2003. Another CD, *Beyond the Sound Barrier*, won a Grammy for Best Instrumental Jazz Album in 2005. In 2006, the Quartet won the 2006 Jazz Journalists' Award for Best Small Ensemble. The Quartet won another Grammy in 2019 for Best Instrumental Jazz Album for the CD/Vinyl album/illustrated book *EMANON*.

In 2015, John, Danilo Perez and Brian Blade released their first recording, *Children of the Light*, also the name of their new trio. Children of the Light toured extensively over the next few years.

John has always felt a call to mentor and teach young musicians and to help further and sustain the art of jazz and bass playing around the world. In 2002, following the retirement of Ron Carter, John began teaching at The City College of New York and was a Professor of Jazz Studies there for ten years. He has also been involved with the Betty Carter Jazz Ahead program in Washington, D.C. and the Thelonious Monk Institute of Jazz. John is a frequent clinician and guest lecturer at schools around the world and a regular featured performer at the International Society of Bassists conventions. In 2010, John began his involvement with the Berklee College of Music's Global Jazz Institute, spearheaded by pianist Danilo Perez. He is currently a Visiting Scholar at Berklee, teaching in both the Global Jazz Institute and the Bass Department.

John currently resides in New York with his wife Sachi, a cellist, and their two daughters.

Introduction

In any kind of jazz setting, whether it's old school or a more modern expression of the form, the role and contribution of the bass player is vital in laying down a foundation for the music. We all know that *what* the bassist plays and *how,* can radically affect the feel and groove of a tune. But the bassist can also change the harmonic structure and mood of a tune through their note choices and rhythmic variations.

When creating basslines in jazz, we need to be aware of both these aspects. Our aim is not simply to find any means to connect the chords and navigate the changes. Instead, we need to think *compositionally*. When we play a bassline, our focus should be on composing a line that is a strong melodic statement in its own right. Then, it must be carried forward with a powerful sense of groove and swing. In this book, I want to share some insights on how to achieve this and teach you some of my jazz vocabulary. My aim is to help you become a great bass *composer* and to improve your sense of groove and swing.

To do this, we will take one of the most common chord sequences in jazz, which appears in hundreds of tunes in the standard repertoire. You'll learn many melodic basslines that work well over this sequence, even when the chords have been significantly altered from their original form.

Composing well-formed, melodic basslines is a lifetime's vocation – and I'm still working on it myself! I have to pay homage here to Ron Carter and Ray Brown. When I first heard those guys playing walking basslines I told myself, "I have to learn how to do *that!*" I also acknowledge the influence of Rufus Reid, another fine bassist who mentored me and helped me on my way. That said, I trust the ideas offered here will help you to grow as a musician and inspire you toward further exploration and creativity. The ultimate aim is to help you find your own voice on the instrument.

This book is based on a simple ii V I VI7 progression in the key of D Major:

| Em7 | A7 | Dmaj7 | B7 |

Beginning with this basic form, the chapters that follow will show you how to adapt your basslines when the harmony is altered in various ways. There are 15 incremental variations of these changes and, as the book progresses, the harmony becomes more colorful and complex. At the beginning of each section you will find a breakdown explaining what changes have been made to the sequence and why these harmonic choices work.

As well as learning dozens of melodic basslines, the narrative will give you an insight into many of the devices commonly used in modern jazz – ways of enriching the changes, and introducing new ones, to open up new possibilities for melodic and rhythmic improvisation.

In every successive section, the chord changes will contain more altered and extended notes and will gravitate further away from the "traditional" changes we'll begin with. By the end, we will be thinking more modally about the chords, viewing each bar as a tonal center in its own right.

This approach should prepare you to play effectively over a large spectrum of the jazz repertoire, from old to new, but it will also help you to quickly decode complex looking chord sequences and better understand how they were constructed.

In each chapter, I present a 32-bar etude comprised of melodic basslines that show how to navigate the changes. The first eight examples are written more simply, striking the middle ground between upright and electric bass.

The final example presents the etude as I would play it if someone handed me a chart of the chord changes on the bandstand. Here, I have added more grace notes, ghost notes, and other inflections that express the language of upright bass and add to the groove and swing. The simpler phrases will help you to lock in the ideas of the guiding principles and prepare you to play the more challenging final etude.

On the next page you'll find instructions on how to download the free audio examples that accompany this book. Be sure to get them, as hearing exactly how each example sounds will enhance your learning experience.

Let's get started!

John.

Get the Audio

The audio files for this book are available to download for free from **www.fundamental-changes.com.** The link is in the top right-hand corner. Click on the "Guitar" link then simply select this book title from the drop-down menu and follow the instructions to get the audio.

We recommend that you download the files directly to your computer, not to your tablet, and extract them there before adding them to your media library. You can then put them onto your tablet, iPod or burn them to CD. On the download page there are instructions and we also provide technical support via the contact form.

For over 350 free guitar lessons with videos check out:

www.fundamental-changes.com

Over 13,000 fans on Facebook: **FundamentalChangesInGuitar**

Tag us for a share on Instagram: **FundamentalChanges**

Understanding Two-Beat Feel

There are two sections to every chapter in this book. The first section presents ideas played with a two-beat feel and the second features conventional walking basslines.

"Playing in two" dates back to the earliest pioneers of jazz. In simple terms, instead of playing a walking bassline with a note for every beat of the bar, two-beat feel emphasizes beats one and three. Later, as jazz evolved and the other instruments (especially the drums) began to emphasize the two and four of the groove, taking this approach on bass created space while still allowing the music to swing. As jazz has continued to develop over the years, modern jazz bass players no longer restrict themselves to playing exclusively on beats one and three, but will generally play half time and punctuate their basslines with melodic phrases and fills.

Playing with a two-beat feel tends to work well when playing the head of a tune, as it allows the melody room to breathe. It also gives the jazz ensemble somewhere to go when they begin soloing and the bassist plays walking patterns. Two-beat feel can also be used effectively on AABA form tunes (such as Rhythm Changes), where the A sections are played half time and the B section follows a walking pattern.

Two-beat feel has been an important feature of the playing of all the greats. Players like Ray Brown and Ron Carter inspired me, spicing up their two-beat feel playing by incorporating chromatic passing notes, interval skips, hammer-ons and pull-offs and other embellishments. Israel Crosby, Paul Chambers, Jimmy Garrison and Dave Holland were also influential in my playing. Bassists like Scott LaFaro and Eddie Gomez (another huge influence for me), who played very freely in the Bill Evans Trio, had the grounding influence of players like Ray Brown, who preceded them, while still forging their own path.

Playing two-beat effectively requires us to develop a great sense of time, feel, groove and swing. While it is difficult to define groove and swing, everyone knows when it's happening! It's often easier to lay down the time when walking four-to-the bar, and harder when there is a lot of space. To help sharpen your skills in this area, I've included two exercises you can build into your practice routine.

Exercise 1 features a simple two-beat bassline that moves through the ii V sequence in all twelve keys. To begin with, set a metronome to a modest tempo that you can easily manage. As you play through the exercise, it's important to focus on both note choice, time and feel. But prioritize the *time* and *feel* more than the notes being played. You might have all the right notes under your fingers, but without great time and feel, your basslines will sound lifeless.

Work with the metronome. The sense of swing in jazz is created by the subtle pulling and pushing of the triplet feel (originally coming from the 6/8 feeling in African music). This triplet feel makes each beat feel wider and leaves room for some notes to be phrased behind the beat, and others in front of it. Hitting every note in a vertical, "quantized" way can feel a little too stiff, but if you explore the wider triplet feel, you might even get your metronome to start to swing!

At face value, Exercise 1 may appear rudimental, but if you can't make the half notes swing, then you will struggle to make the quarter notes swing.

Exercise 1

Another important part of two-beat feel is incorporating triplet phrases. After we've played simple root notes on beats one and three, a fast triplet phrase can provide contrast and movement. Triplet phrases can be placed on any beat of the bar, and you can include more than one in a bar to create a burst of intensity before returning to a more spacious, straightforward feel.

Based on the previous exercise, Exercise 2 cycles through all 12 keys with a two-beat feel and triplet embellishments. Be sure to play these at a comfortable tempo to begin with, so that you fully articulate the lines with a deep sense of swing. Record yourself and listen back to see if it *feels* right to you or not. Also go and listen to some of the recordings made by the great bassists I mentioned earlier. The more you listen, the more that sense of swing will become ingrained.

When playing this exercise, continue to concentrate on time and feel. Don't speed up your metronome until you've nailed the right feel at a slower tempo.

Exercise 2

Do make sure you give enough time to these exercises before moving on. Make them part of your warm-up routine before you play. For variety, you can adapt the exercise to include some chromatic movements or sequential movements in minor thirds. Also, practice two-beat feel with triplets over the changes to some of your favorite standard tunes.

Chapter One: ii V I VI7

Guiding principles

Before you play the melodic basslines I've composed for you, I want to lay down some guiding principles to bear in mind when working through this material. These will be especially important when you set out to compose your own basslines. Of course, the nature of music and particularly jazz harmony is a fluid thing, so even if we have rules, we can always break them. But if you follow these principles you will have a strong foundation to work from and you will develop the skill of composing more interesting and more melodic basslines, while prioritizing a strong time feel. In essence, here is a summary of how I think when composing basslines.

Principle #1

Rhythmic integrity, swing and variety are extremely important.

All the "right" notes but executed without the right rhythmic feel and swinging inflections results in *ineffective bass playing!*

Principle #2

Foundational notes are always more important than alterations.

The role of the bass player has always been to provide a strong harmonic foundation – and that's still your job! The fundamental tones that define a chord are the bass player's starting point: the root, 3rd, 5th and 7th. In jazz, the ii V sequence, minor to dominant 7th, is so ubiquitous that you must know the root, 5th, b7 and octave to define those minor and dominant chords which are so common.

Just because a chord progression contains a lot of altered and extended chords, it doesn't mean the bassist has to include *all* those alterations in their lines. This is especially important if the extensions/alterations are above the octave, such as the b9, #9, 11, #11, 13 and b13. If the bassist is playing these notes, say in the lower register, there may be a perceived disconnect from the fundamental harmony.

Principle #3

When composing basslines, start simple, then add layers of complexity.

Never lose sight of the fact that you're playing a song, not engaging in a technical exercise. Even when you play a scale, you should make it sound like it is the most beautiful piece of music you ever heard! Begin with simple arpeggios, then add scale tones. The next layer is to use approach notes and chromatic passing tones, but with care.

Principle #4

Compose lines that have interest and movement.

Bearing in mind all of the above, to compose basslines that have movement but retain melodic integrity, you can use these additional tools:

- Broken 3rds, 4ths, 5ths, 6ths, 7ths and octaves

- Four-note patterns ascending and descending with symmetrical shapes

- Patterns that move in and out of the harmony, as long as the patterns have a discernable logic to them

I always try to point students toward the idea of becoming a storyteller. When you're having a conversation with someone, you may exchange a few words, then one person will say something that builds into a longer sentence. From there it might develop into a few sentences, and so on.

When composing on bass, you can start with a few words – a simple motif. Then you can develop that thought into a sentence. From there, the idea might grow into a paragraph, and several paragraphs begin to tell a story. The point is: the story grows organically from the starting motif. Every new idea is built on the previous one.

With this fundamental idea in mind, let's move on to play through the basic chord sequence that forms the foundation of this book. Remember, the progressions in the subsequent chapters are all variations of these changes.

Chord sequence:

| Em7 | A7 | Dmaj7 | B7 |

Sequence overview:

We are working in the key of D Major. Below are the notes of the D Major scale and underneath, the chords that are produced when the scale is harmonized.

Harmonizing notes to produce a chord simply means to take a note then stack intervals of a 3rd on top (every other note). The Dmaj7 chord is therefore constructed D – F# – A – C#

After each chord name is a Roman numeral which describes its place in the scale. Jazz musicians make great use of this system to quickly describe a set of chord changes (such as I vi ii V in Bb, for instance – the beginning of a Rhythm Changes tune). This information immediately conveys what chords are to be played.

D	E	F#	G	A	B	C#
Dmaj7 (I)	Em7 (ii)	F#m7 (iii)	Gmaj7 (IV)	A7 (V)	Bmin7 (vi)	C#m7b5 (vii)

In bar 4 of our sequence we see the first common jazz harmony alteration. Jazz musicians will often change the *quality* of certain chords in a sequence. Typically, this will be to change the original chord into a dominant, so here B7 is played in place of Bm7. The reason for this is that dominant chords can be altered in various ways to include tension notes, and this gives improvisers more scale options when soloing. We'll explore this concept more as we progress.

Listen to the audio examples and then play through each of the two-beat feel examples.

Two-Beat Feel Examples

Example 1a

Example 1b

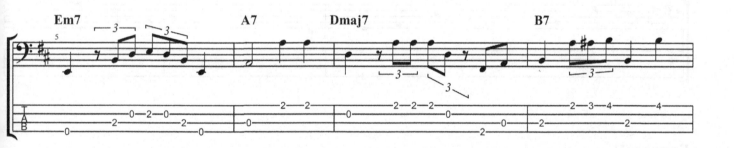

Example 1c

Example 1d

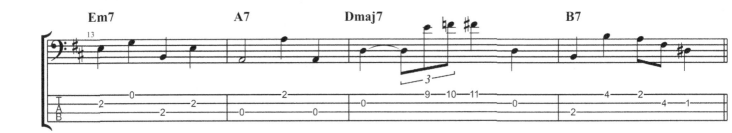

Notice that, where possible, when playing upright I will always use the open strings to play a note. This helps with economy of motion for the left hand. Later, when you play across more of the range of the fingerboard/ fretboard, open strings are also useful to make transitions between positions sound seamless. Feel free to adapt this if playing electric.

Now play through the following walking examples.

Walking Examples

Example 1e

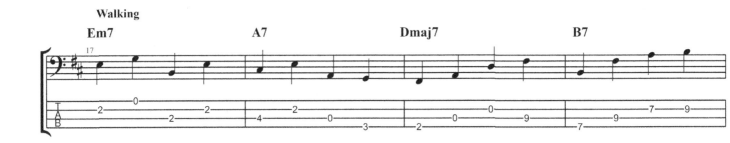

Example 1f

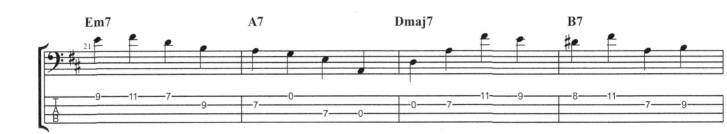

Example 1g

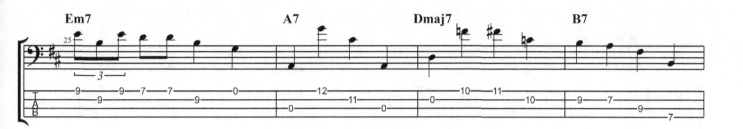

Example 1h

Having worked through these four-bar phrases, now you are prepared to tackle the final etude, which as added embellishments, and moves from two-beat feel to walking.

Example 1i

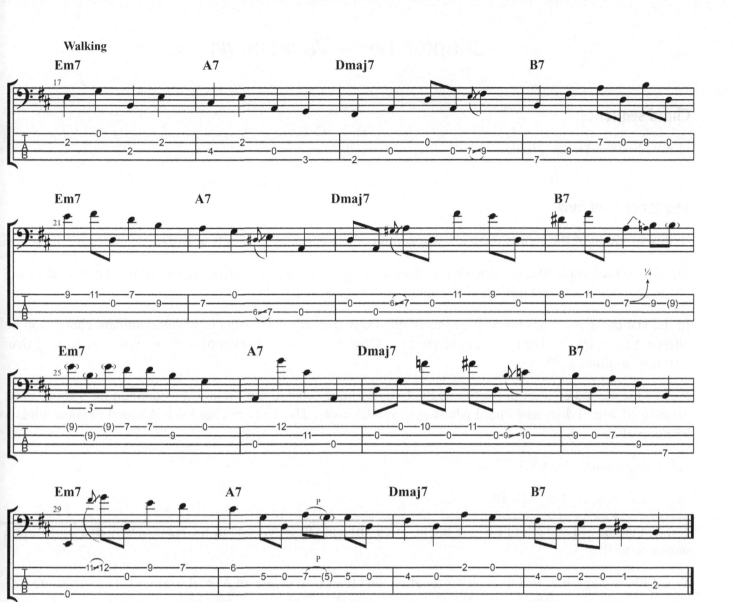

Chapter Two – Variation #1

Chord sequence:

| Em9 | Eb7#9 | Dmaj9 | B7#5 |

Sequence overview:

In this variation of the chords there are two common jazz harmony concepts at work.

The first is the simple idea of enriching the harmony by extending or altering chords. In this version, the Em7 has been extended to an Em9. Similarly, Dmaj7 is changed to Dmaj9.

In the last bar, the B7 has been altered to B7#5. There are only four ways in which dominant chords can be altered: b5, #5, b9, #9. The use of the #5 creates a tension that makes the chord want to resolve even more than a straight dominant 7th.

We see the second concept in bar two: a flat five or tritone substitution. In jazz it's common for a chord to be substituted with a dominant chord whose root is a b5 away. The original chord was A7, and the note Eb is a b5 interval above A.

A7 is constructed: A – C# – E – G

Eb7 is constructed: Eb – G – Bb – Db

Notice that the 3rd and 7th of Eb7 are the inverted 3rd and 7th of A7, one of the reasons why this substitution works so well.

When Eb7 is superimposed over an A7 tonality, the effect is to create an A7b5(b9) sound. The substitute Eb7 chord has also been altered to add the #9 tension note (F#). The F# is a note it shares with Em9, making the transition from one chord to the next sound smoother.

Here are the two-beat feel examples.

Two-Beat Feel Examples

Example 2a

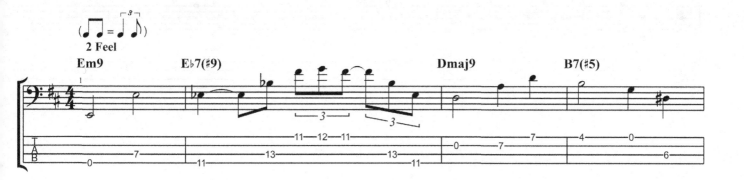

Example 2b

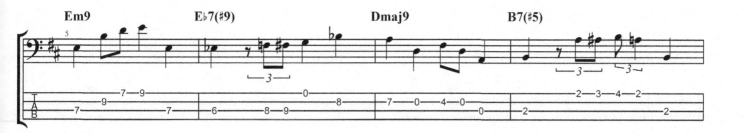

Example 2c

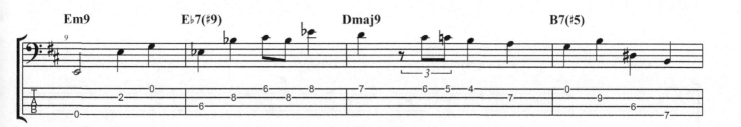

Example 2d

Now play through the walking examples.

Walking Examples

Example 2e

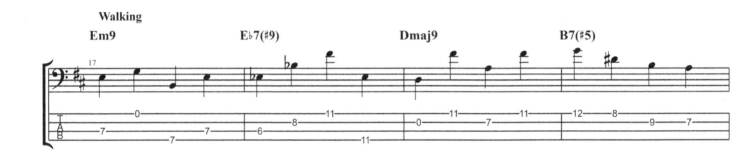

Example 2f

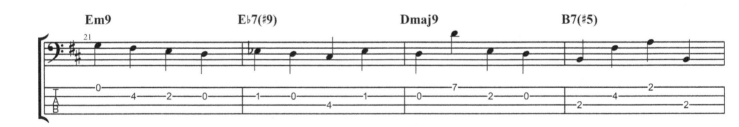

Example 2g

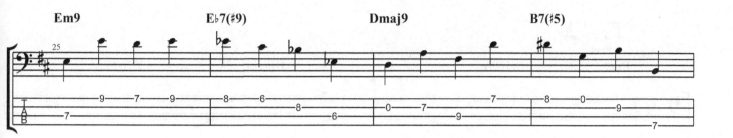

Example 2h

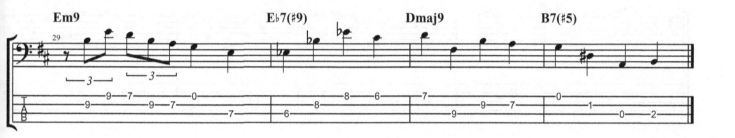

Next, play through the full etude.

Example 2i

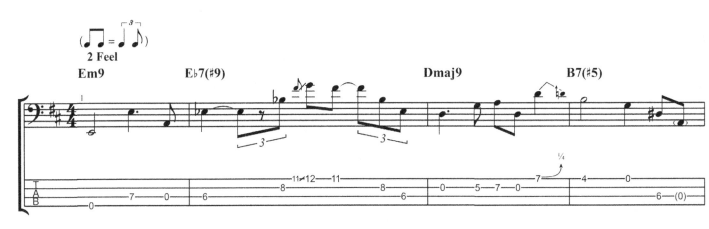

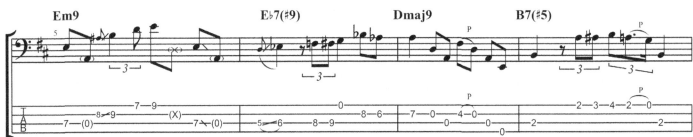

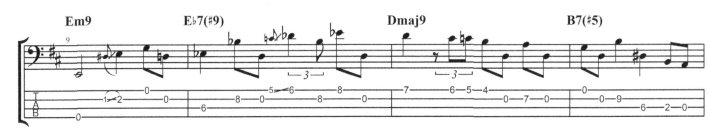

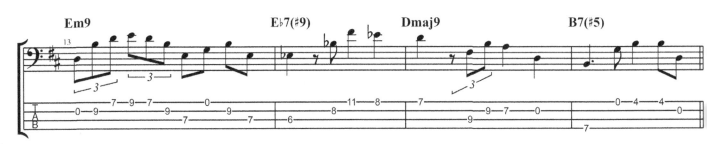

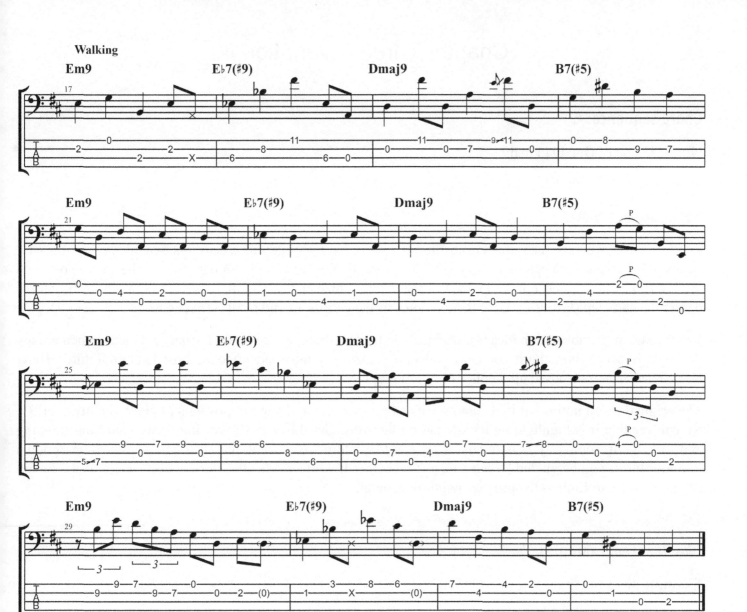

Chapter Three – Variation #2

Chord sequence:

| Em9 | Eb7#11 | Dmaj9 | Fmaj9 |

Sequence overview:

In this version, we have the same b5 substitution idea in bar two, but with a different extended note – the #11. One way of voicing the chords in bars 1-2 is to place the 9th (F#) as the highest note in the Em9 chord, and the 3rd (G) as the highest note in Eb7#11. This creates a nice contrary motion as the bass notes of the chords descend a half step (E to Eb), while the top notes of the chords ascend a half step (F# to G).

In bar four a new substitution idea is introduced. In jazz harmony it's common for musical ideas (whether they be single-line melodies, chords, or chord cadences such as ii V movements) to be shifted in minor thirds. Here, Dmaj9 has been transposed up a minor third to Fmaj9.

The original chord in this bar is B7, and if we analyze the effect of superimposing an Fmaj9 tonality over B7, we can see that it is highlighting b5, #5 and b9 tensions. But this way of viewing it can cloud our thinking and stifle the freedom of jazz harmony. It's easier to explore the concept that ideas can be moved up or down in minor thirds and be guided by our ears as to whether it works musically. Here it works well, as the Fmaj9 resolves nicely to Em9 as the progression turns around.

Two-Beat Feel Examples

Example 3a

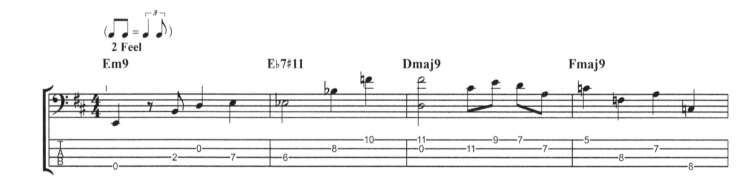

Example 3b

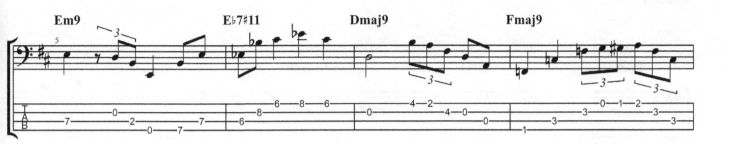

Example 3c

Example 3d

Now here are the walking bassline examples.

Walking Examples

Example 3e

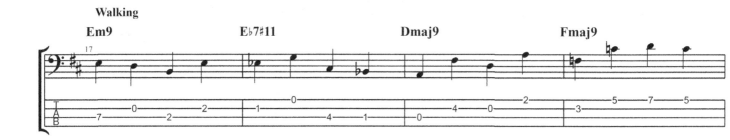

Example 3f

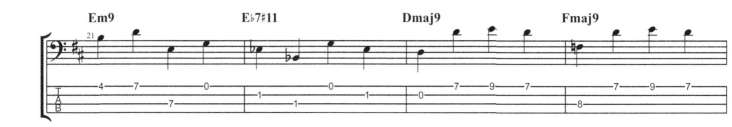

Example 3g

Example 3h

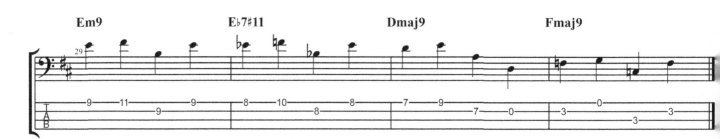

Now play through the full etude focusing on keeping good time and feel.

Example 3i

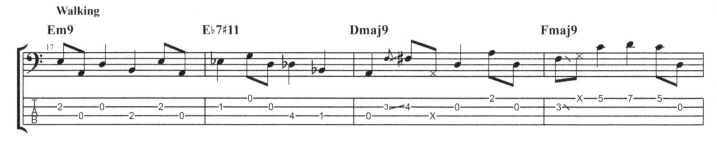

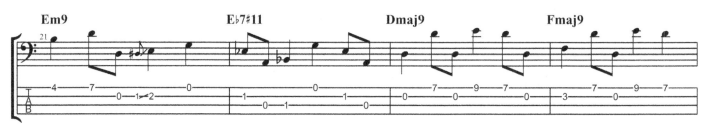

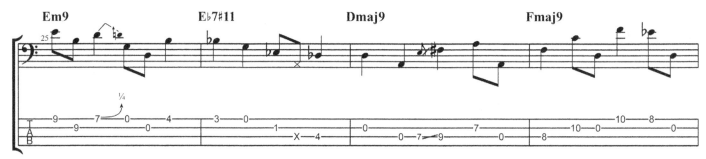

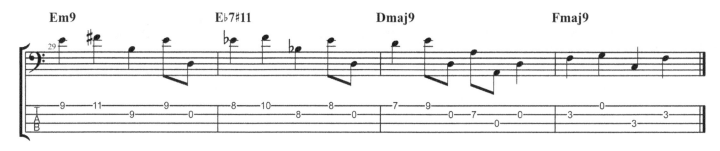

Chapter Four – Variation #3

Chord sequence:

| Em11 | Bbm9 Eb9 | Dmaj9 Bm9 | B7#5 |

Sequence overview:

In bar one, Em7 is replaced with the more open-sounding Em11.

In bar two, we have the b5 substitution again (Eb9 in place of A7). This time, however, we see a common bebop device: every dominant chord in a progression is viewed as a V chord and preceded by its ii chord. Bbm9 and Eb9 are the ii and V chords in the key of Ab Major. Even though the target tonality we are aiming for is D Major in bar three, the substitute ii V sequence gives soloists the option of improvising briefly in Ab Major in bar two, before resolving to D Major.

In bar three, the Bm9 is added to complement the Dmaj9 and introduce a different color. A pianist or guitarist might choose to play a rootless Bm9 here, as with the B root it has the exact same notes as Dmaj7. Alternatively, you could choose to make a feature of the B in the bass, as it would anticipate the B7#5 and act like a pedal tone.

Two-Beat Feel Examples

Example 4a

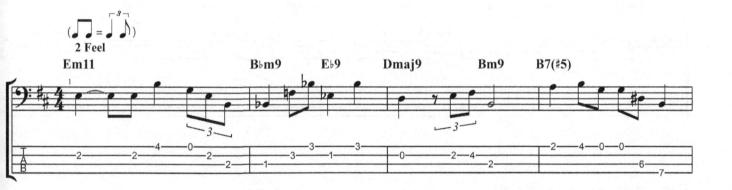

Example 4b

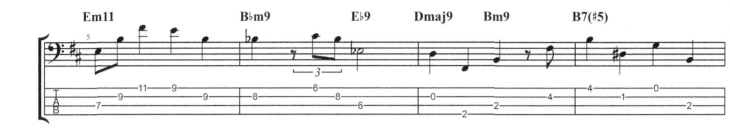

Example 4c

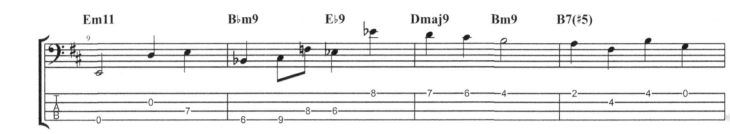

Example 4d

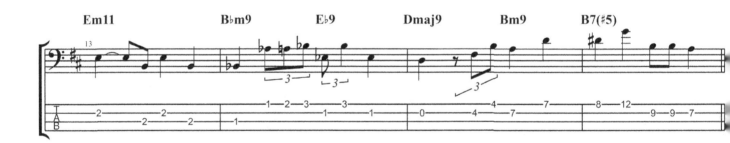

Here are the walking variations.

Walking Examples

Example 4e

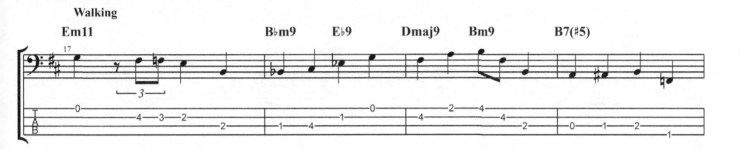

Example 4f

Example 4g

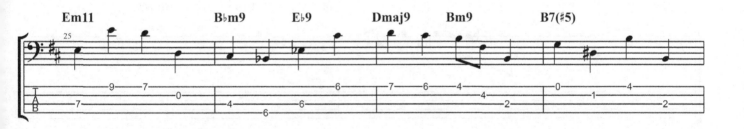

Example 4h

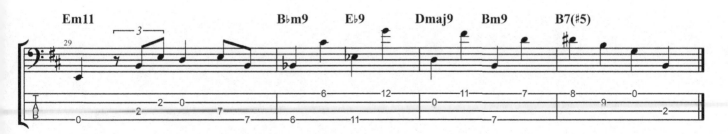

And now, the enhanced etude.

Example 4i

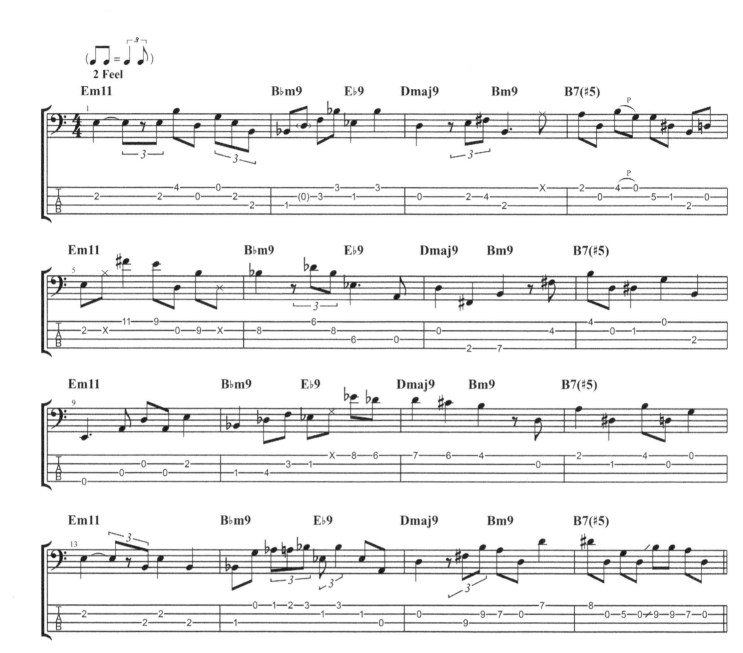

Walking

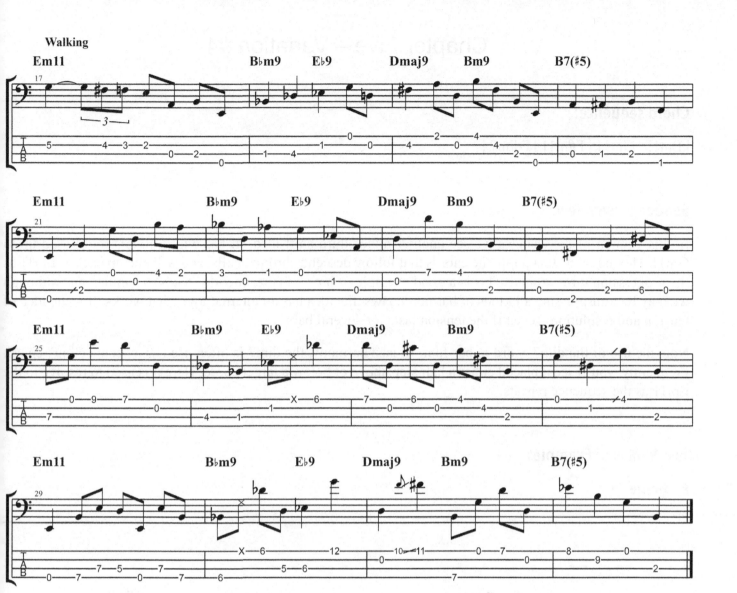

Chapter Five – Variation #4

Chord sequence:

| Em11 | Gm11 | F#m11 | Fdim7 |

Sequence overview:

In this version of the changes we see another minor third shift idea. In bar two, Em11 is transposed up to Gm11. Having made that jump, the chords that follow descend chromatically, and will end up back at Em11 as the progression turns around. This is a good example of how, in jazz, one idea leads to another, and although we may be transgressing all kinds of harmonic laws, the idea has an internal logic that works. It is the idea of tension and resolution – even if the tension lasts for several bars.

Note the use of the dim7 chord in bar four. In jazz harmony, the dim7 is often used as a "connecting" chord. Frequently, you'll see it placed either a half step above or below a target chord. Here it is used to resolve to the Em11 as the sequence repeats.

Two-Beat Feel Examples

Example 5a

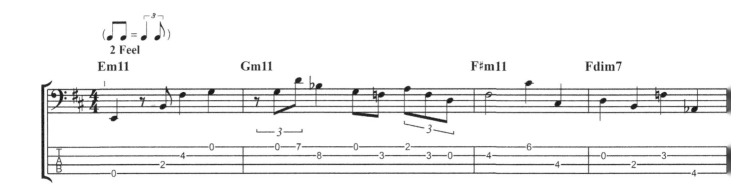

Example 5b

Example 5c

Example 5d

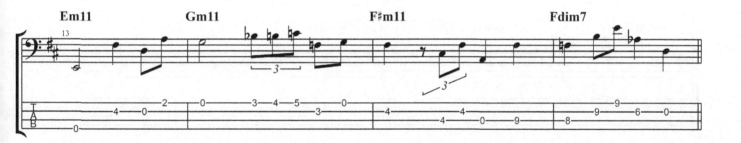

Now work through the walking examples.

Walking Examples

Example 5e

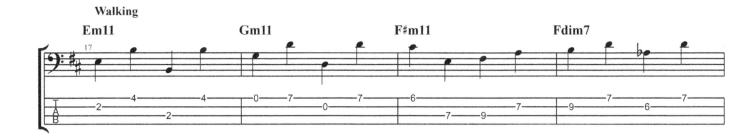

Example 5f

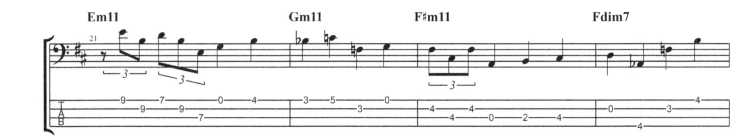

Example 5g

Example 5h

Here is the full etude.

Example 5i

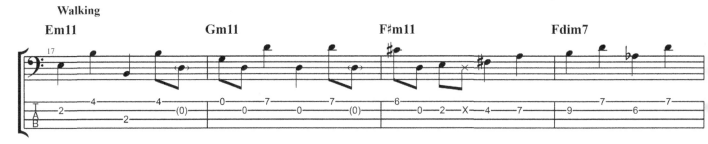

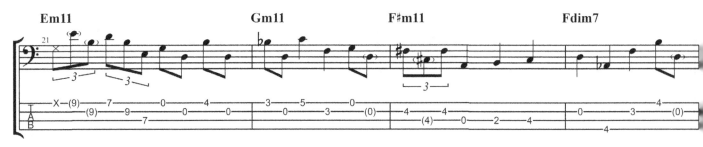

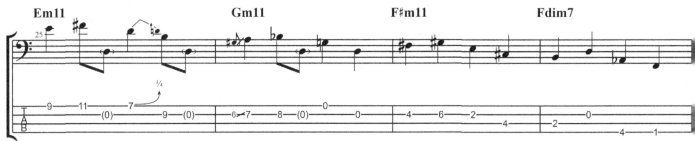

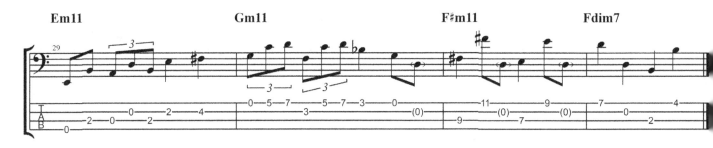

Chapter Six – Variation #5

Chord sequence:

| Em7 A7 | Gm7 C13 | Dmaj7 G9 | F#m7 B7#5 |

Sequence overview:

Here is another variation of the minor third shift. Jazz musicians will often play a "quick" ii V in order to add another ii V a minor third away into a sequence. The Em7 to A7 cadence that normally spans two bars has been "compressed" into one bar, so that the additional ii V (Gm7 – C13) can be played in bar two.

In bar four, the ii chord of B7 has been added, bebop style, to create more movement. The G9 chord at the end of bar three was added as a way of navigating smoothly from Dmaj7 to the F#m7.

Two-Beat Feel Examples

Example 6a

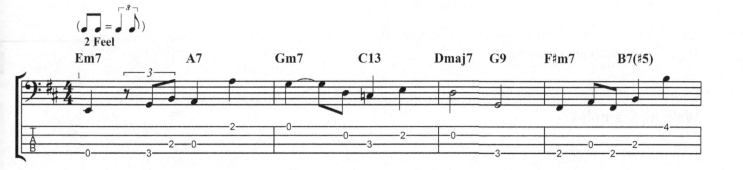

Example 6b

Example 6c

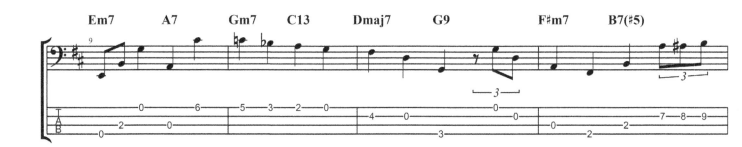

Example 6d

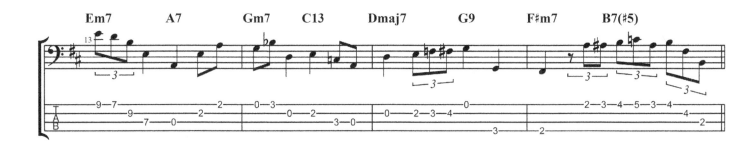

Here are the walking examples.

Walking Examples

Example 6e

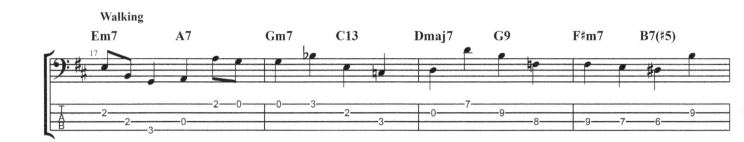

Example 6f

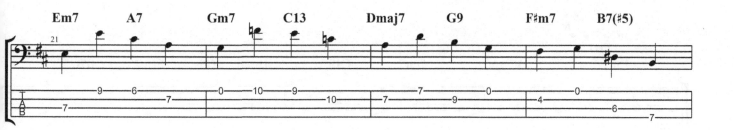

Example 6g

Example 6h

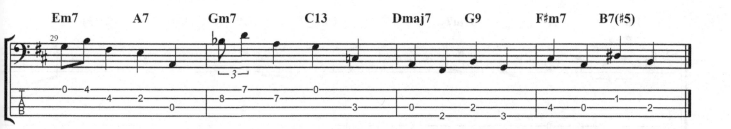

Now play through the etude with added embellishments.

Example 6i

Chapter Seven – Variation #6

Chord sequence:

| Em11 A13 | Bbm7 Eb7 | Dmaj7 Gmaj9 | F#m7 F13#11 |

Sequence overview:

This iteration of the chord changes combines several ideas we've discussed so far. In bar one, the Em7 to A7 cadence is compressed and the chords have been extended to add color. In bar two, we have the b5 substitution. Eb7 replaces A7 and is preceded by its ii chord. In bar three, the Dmaj7 to Gmaj9 is a chord I to chord IV movement.

In bar four, the chords are descending chromatically from Gmaj9, heading for the target chord of Em11 as the progression turns around. The F#m7 chord is straightforward, but the F13#11 presents us with some interesting melodic options.

Technically, F13#11 is a seven-note voicing if you include all the notes, and is constructed:

F (root), A (3rd), C (5th), Eb (b7), G (9th), B (#11), D (13th)

But practically, it is more common to play it as a five-note chord: F – Eb – G – B – D

This means that we could view the chord as a shell voicing of F7 (F and Eb, the root and b7), with a G Major triad on top (G, B and D). The polytonal nature of the chord opens up the possibility of briefly playing notes from a G Major tonality.

That said, we must remember the guiding principle of the bass player. Just because those tensions exist in the chords, we don't *have* to highlight them.

Two-Beat Feel Examples

Example 7a

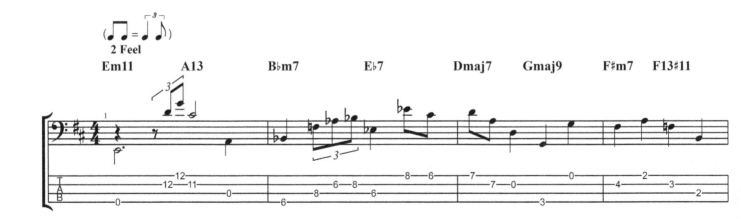

Example 7b

Example 7c

Example 7d

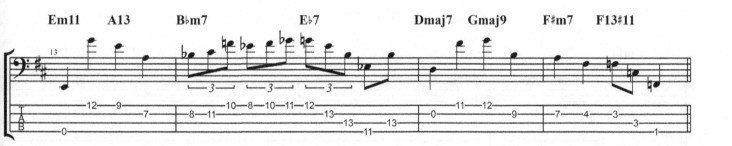

Now try these walking examples.

Walking Examples

Example 7e

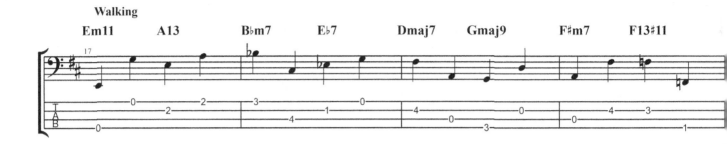

Example 7f

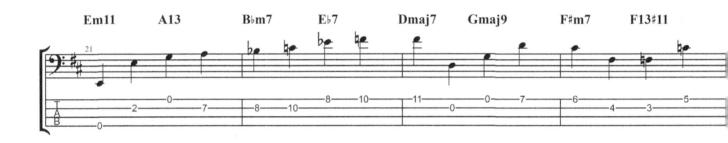

Example 7g

Example 7h

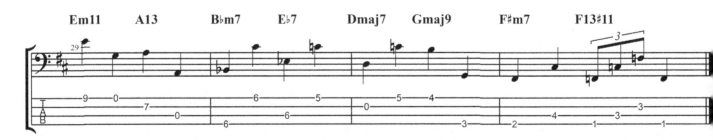

Now try the full etude.

Example 7i

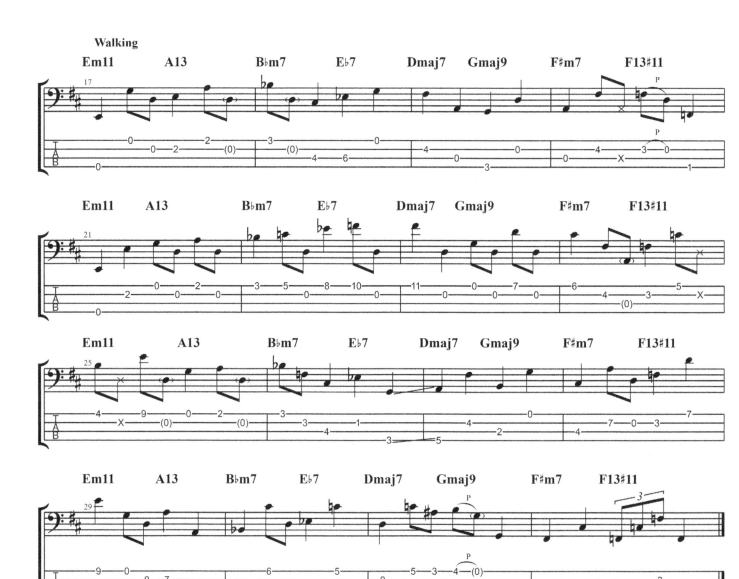

Chapter Eight – Variation #7

Chord sequence:

| Em11 | A7b5 | Dmaj7#11 Gmaj7#11 | F#m11 Fmaj7#11 |

Sequence overview:

In this harmonization of the changes, in bar two there is the simple idea of adding an alteration to the A7 chord (the b5) that begs to be resolved. The sequence that follows has the same approach we've used before – a chord I to chord IV shift (from D to G) followed by a chromatic descent. The difference here is the extensive use of angular sounding #11 chords.

In bar four, the F#m11 can be voiced F# – B – E – A and the Fmaj7#11 voiced F – B – E – A. This makes for a very smooth transition as they have only one note different. Fmaj7#11 resolves nicely to Em11 to circle around the progression.

Two-Beat Feel Examples

Example 8a

Example 8b

Example 8c

Example 8d

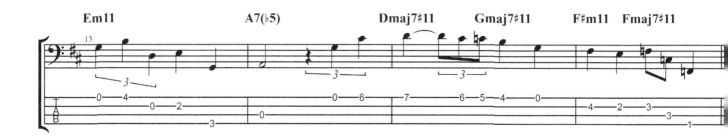

Here are the walking examples for this sequence.

Walking Examples

Example 8e

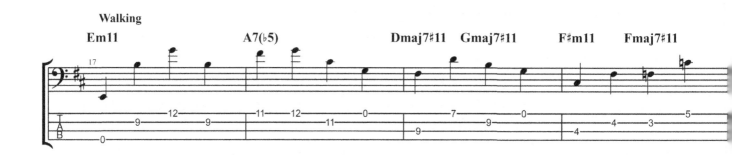

Example 8f

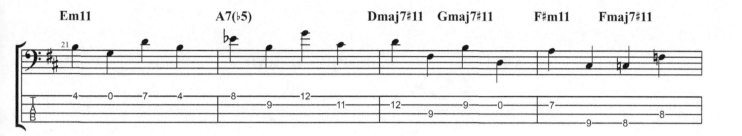

Example 8g

Example 8h

Here is the full etude.

Example 8i

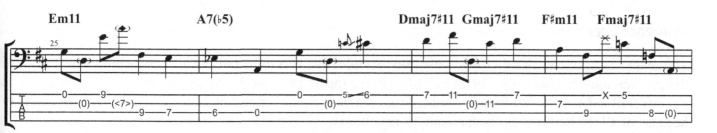

Chapter Nine – Variation #8

Chord sequence:

| Em11 | Bb13 A13 | Eb7#9 Dmaj9 | C13 B7#5 |

Sequence overview:

This expression of the chord changes uses one simple, but very effective idea: approaching each chord in the progression chromatically from a half step above (apart from the Em11 in bar one). This device creates the effect of a constantly shifting harmony. From the bass player's point of view, it's a nice sequence to play because of all the half step shifts that connect the chords.

The extensions and alterations made to the individual chords here are just a matter of taste, based on how much tension and resolution is desired.

Two-Beat Feel Examples

Example 9a

Example 9b

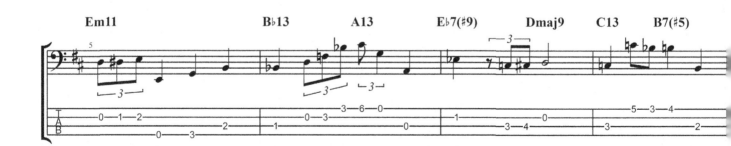

Example 9c

Example 9d

Now, here are the walking examples over these changes.

Walking Examples

Example 9e

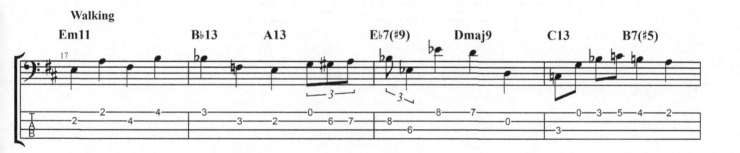

Example 9f

Example 9g

Example 9h

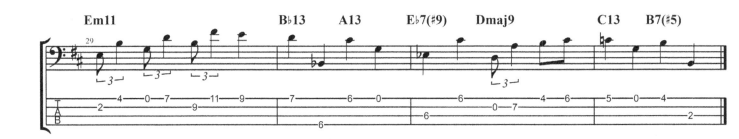

Here is the complete etude.

Example 9i

Chapter Ten – Variation #9

Chord sequence:

| Em11 | Gm11 C13b9 | Bm9 | B7#5b9 |

Sequence overview:

In this variation of the changes, we see the minor third shift in bar two, and here the sequence is turned into a ii V cadence: Gm11 – C13b9. The C dominant chord then leads chromatically to the Bm9 in bar three. Here, if the Bm9 chord is played without its root, it contains identical notes to Dmaj7. The B7 chord in bar four is spiced up with a #5 and b9.

Two-Beat Feel Examples

Example 10a

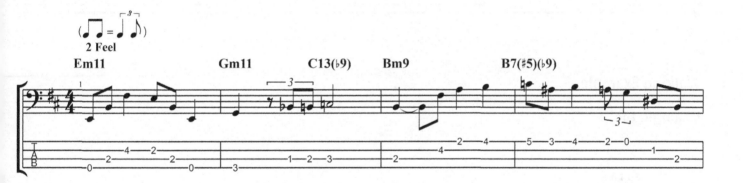

Example 10b

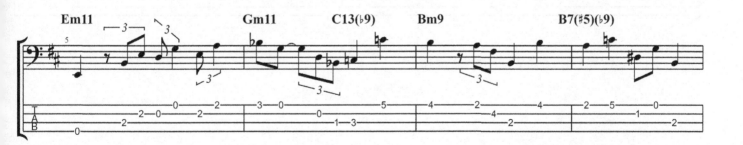

Example 10c

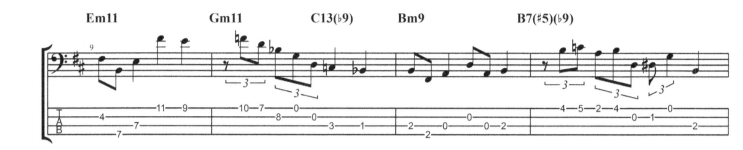

Example 10d

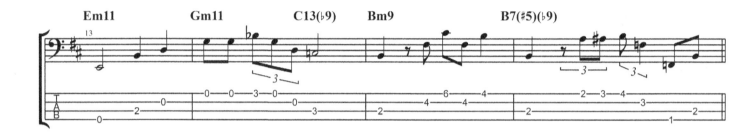

Walking Examples

Example 10e

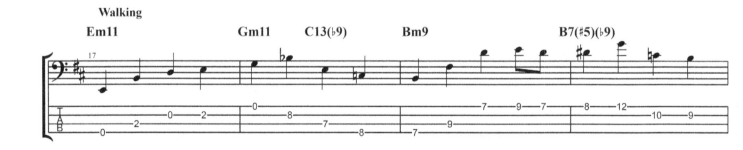

Example 10f

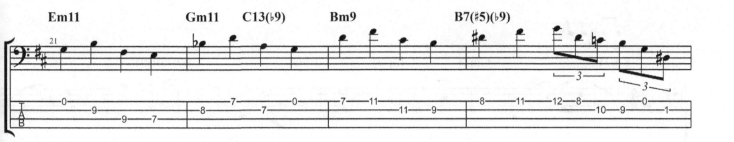

Example10g

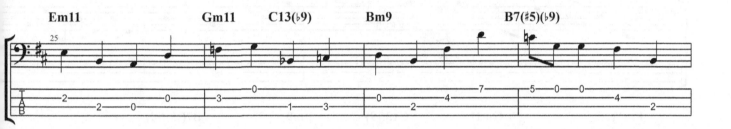

Example 10h

Here is the full etude to play through.

Example 10i

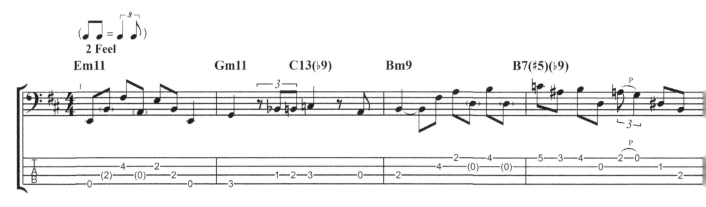

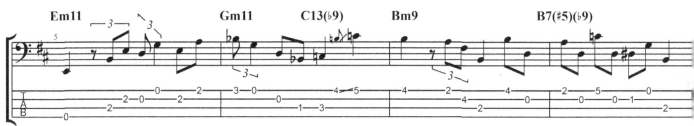

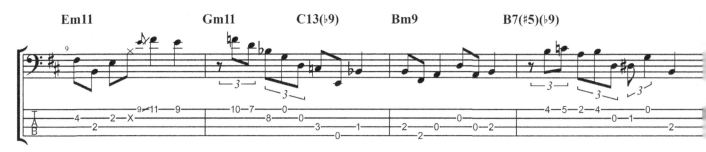

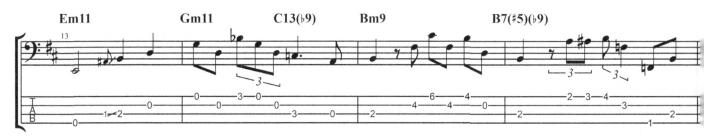

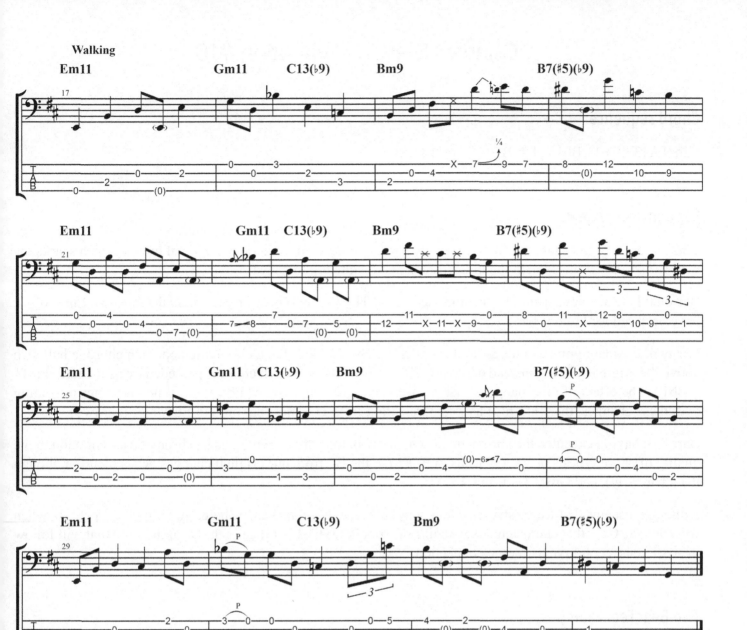

Chapter Eleven – Variation #10

Chord sequence:

| Em9 A13 | Fm11 Bb13 | F#° B7#5 | Gm11 C13 |

Sequence overview:

This variation of the changes offers some new harmonic ideas. It's a good example of how one idea sparks the next in jazz, so let me explain the logical steps that resulted in this idea.

Bar one: here we have a simple "compressed" ii V. The first two bars of our original sequence, Em7 to A7, have been reduced to one bar.

Bar two: the main point of interest in this bar is the Bb13 chord. It's a chromatic approach chord, a half step above the original A7. But instead of playing Bb13 to A7, the approach chord is preceded by its ii chord: Fm11 – Bb13. The effect of this change is that we are fleetingly in the key of Eb Major. When it comes to soloing over these changes, there is a nice half step transition from D Major (bar one) to Eb Major (bar two).

Bars 3-4: having executed the chromatic idea in bar two, the pattern continues its chromatic ascent, though the quality of chord types change. F#° leads to B7#5 (so the B7 from our original changes gets a mention, though it's a bar early), and Gm11 leads to C13.

Although it seems that we've strayed a long way from the original changes here, by following a pattern, when we reach the C13, that chord actually contains the root note (E), b3 (G) and 5th (D) of the Em9 that will follow it, so there is a cohesive harmonic connection.

Two-Beat Feel Examples

Example 11a

Example 11b

Example 11c

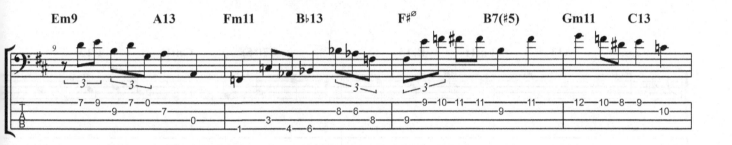

Example 11d

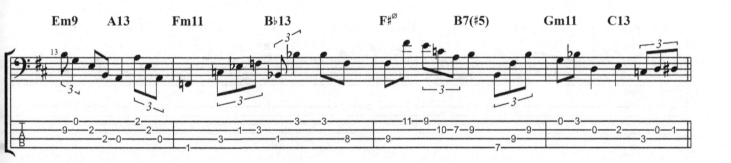

Walking Examples

Example 11e

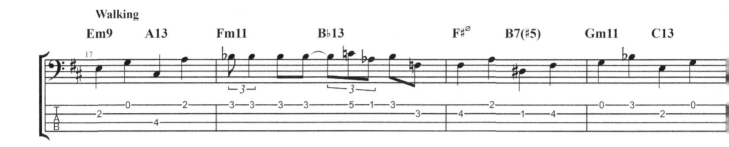

Example 11f

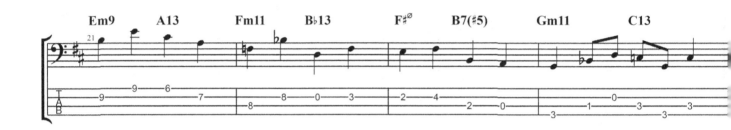

Example 11g

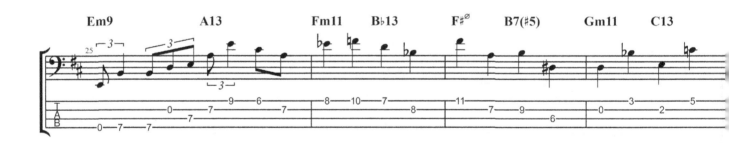

Example 11h

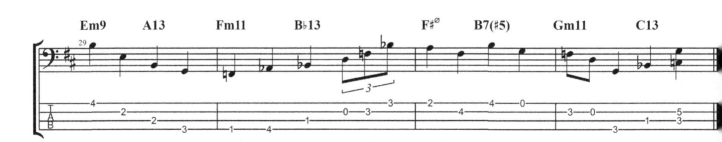

Now play through the full etude.

Example 11i

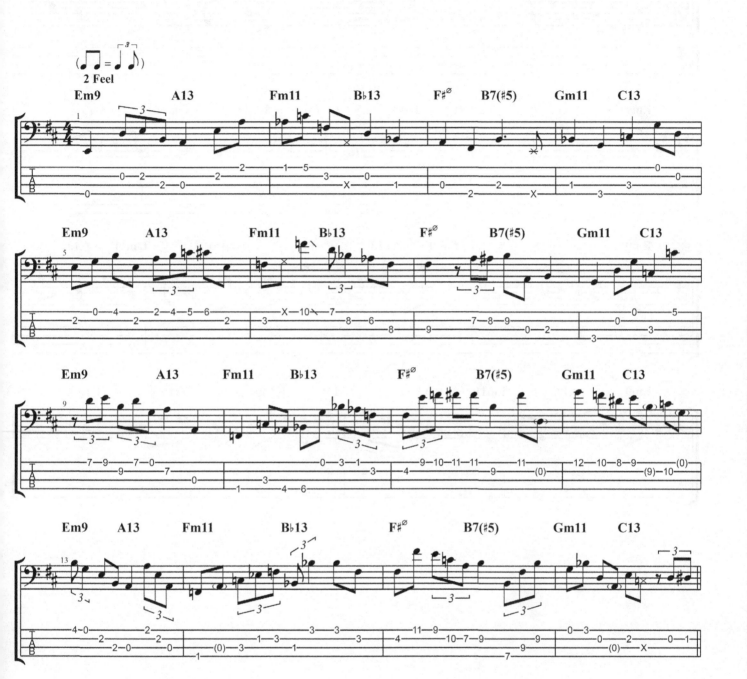

Chapter Twelve – Variation #11

Chord sequence:

| Em9 | Ebmaj9 | Dmaj9 | Fmaj9 |

Sequence overview:

Here is a simple but effective reharmonization of the original sequence. Following on from the Em9 chord in bar one, the Ebmaj9 chord is a b5 substitution for A7. What's unusual is that the quality of the chord has been changed from a dominant 7th to a major 9th. However, another way of looking at the Ebmaj9 is that it is simply a chromatic approach chord, a half step above the Dmaj9. In bar four, we see the familiar minor third shift up to Fmaj9, which will resolve to Em9 to restart the cycle.

Two-Beat Feel Examples

Example 12a

Example 12b

Example 12c

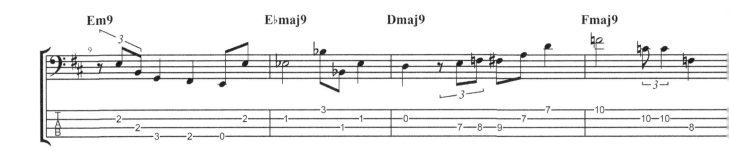

Example 12d

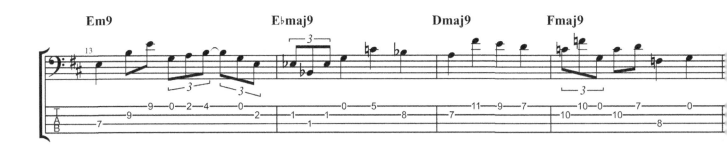

Walking Examples

Example 12e

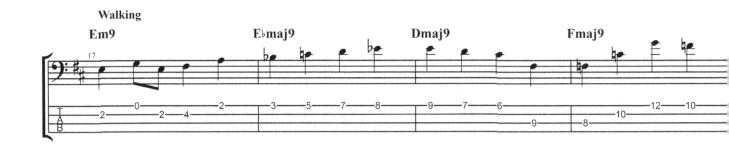

Example 12f

Example 12g

Example 12h

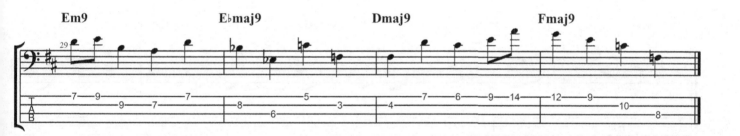

Here is the full etude.

Example 12i

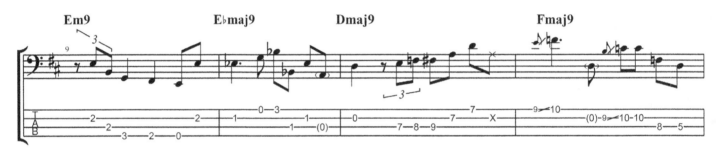

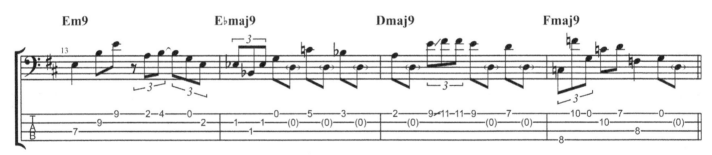

Chapter Thirteen – Variation #12

Chord sequence:

| Gmaj7 | GmMaj7#11 | Dmaj7 G7b5 | F#º B7#9 |

Sequence overview:

In bar one of this version, I've indicated that the chord is Gmaj7, but we know that the original chord is an E minor, and in previous versions we've used Em9 here. If we think of the Em9 as a rootless voicing, without its E bass note it contains the same notes as Gmaj7.

Em9 no root: G (b3), B (5th), D (7th), F# (9th)

Gmaj7: G (root), B (3rd), D (5th), F# (7th)

The interchangeability of Major 7 and rootless minor 9 voicings is a concept jazz pianists/guitarists use to increase the range of available chord voicings. To use this idea, think relative Major/Minor keys (i.e. G Major is the relative Major key of E Minor and vice versa.

The chord in bar two is notated GmMaj7#11. To understand this chord, it's helpful to compare it to the Gmaj7 voicing:

Gmaj7: G – B – D – F#

GmMaj7#11: G – Bb – C# – F#

To create the second chord, two voices (the B and D notes) are lowered a half step, while the others remain the same.

If we were to add the A bass note from the original harmony to the second chord, then we would have an A13b9:

A – G – Bb – C# – F#

But most jazz pianists would simply view this chord as functioning as G diminished. All the notes are contained within the G Whole-Half Diminished scale:

G – A – Bb – C – C# – D# – E – F#

Bar three contains a chord I to chord IV shift from Dmaj7 to G7b5. From the G7b5, the half diminished chord a half step below sets up a ii V movement to land on B7#9.

Two-Beat Feel Examples

Example 13a

Example 13b

Example 13c

Example 13d

Here are the walking bassline examples to work through.

Walking Examples

Example 13e

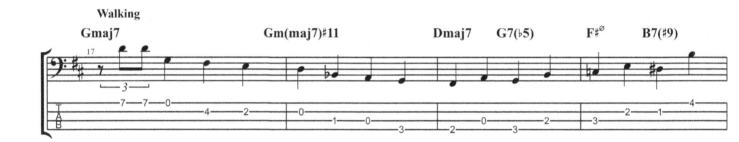

Example 13f

Example 13g

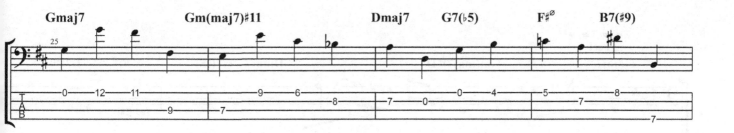

Example 13h

Now here is the full etude.

Example 13i

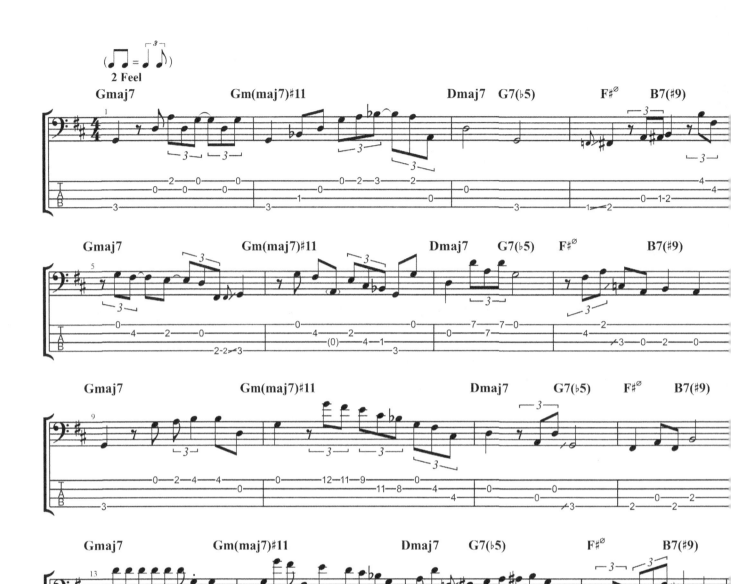

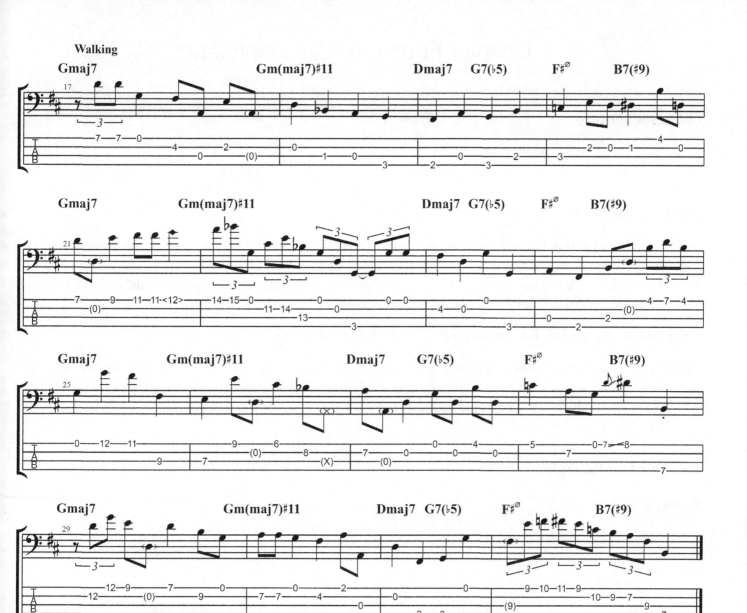

Chapter Fourteen – Variation #13

Chord sequence:

| Em7b5 | Ebmaj7#11 | Dmaj9 | Fmaj7#11 |

Sequence overview:

In this reharmonization, we begin with an Em7b5 chord in place of Em7, as though the progression is a minor ii V i rather than a Major ii V I. Instead of moving to an A7 or A7alt in bar two, however, we have a b5 substitution, this time rendered as Ebmaj7#11. Bar three has a D Major chord type, as in the original changes, then in bar four, the original B7 is replaced with Fmaj7#11.

Fmaj7#11 is constructed: F (root), A (3rd), C (5th), E (7th), B (#11).

The F tonality is a minor third shift from the D tonality of bar three. If we superimposed Fmaj7#11 over a B dominant tonality, however, we'd see that the chord contains the root note (B) and b7 (A), then altered tensions which imply a B7alt chord. The F note suggests the b5, the C note the b9, and the E note the 11th.

Two-Beat Feel Examples

Example 14a

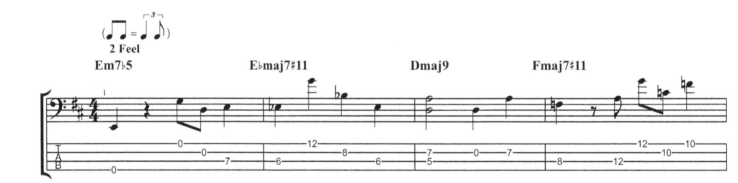

Example 14b

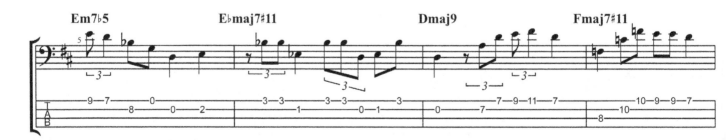

Example 14c

Example 14d

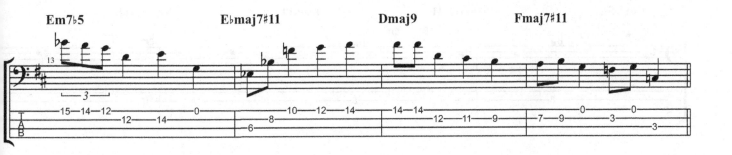

Here are the walking lines.

Walking Examples

Example 14e

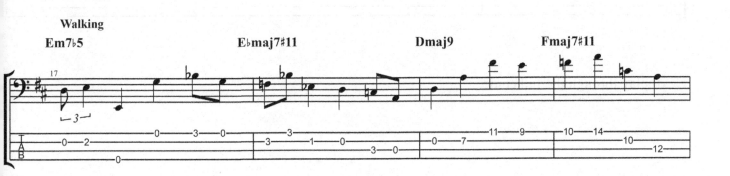

Example14f

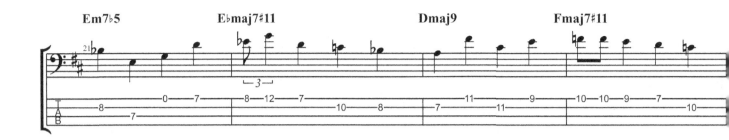

Example 14g

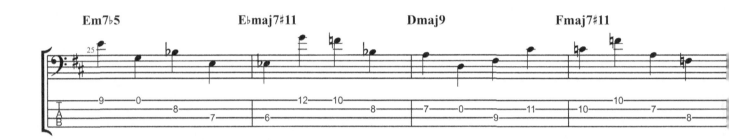

Example 14h

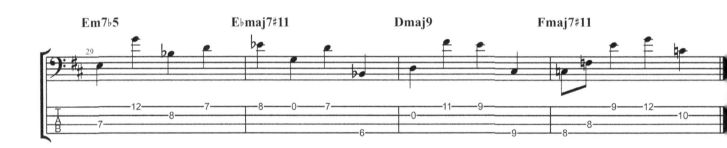

Next, play through the full etude.

Example 14i

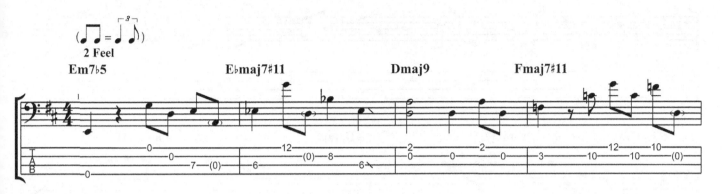

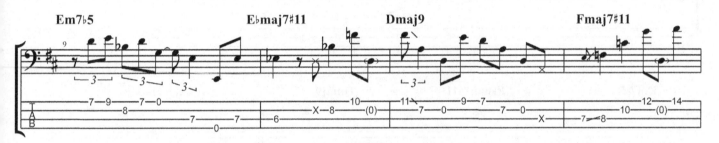

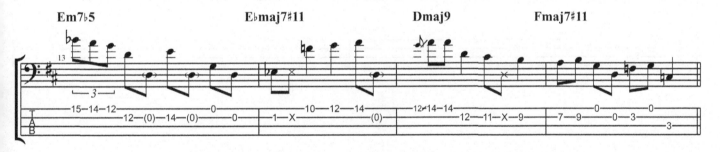

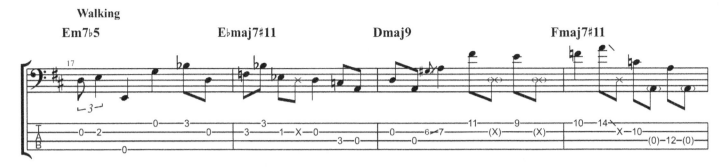

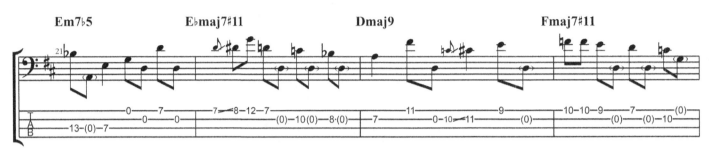

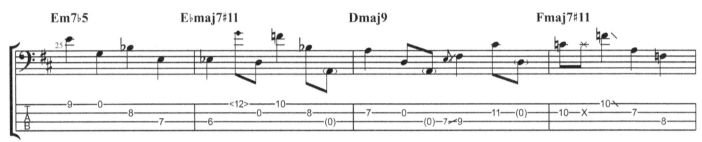

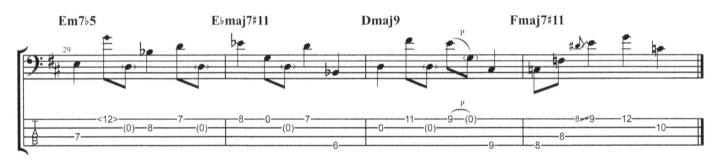

Chapter Fifteen – Variation #14

Chord sequence:

| Bb/E | Eb/A | E/D | F/B |

Sequence overview:

Throughout this book we've adapted the simple ii V I VI7 progression in different ways using a variety of modern jazz harmonic concepts. Now we have the most modal sounding of the variations.

A common feature of modal jazz is the idea of superimposing one tonality over another. Notice in the progression above that the bass notes still spell out the root notes of the ii V I VI7 sequence, but triads have been added on top. At first glance they appear distant from our original harmony. However, let's analyze the chords more closely.

Bb/E

The Bb Major triad contains the notes Bb, D and F. Combined with the E bass note, this chord shares four notes in common with E7(b5b9):

E7(b5b9) = E, G#, Bb, D, F

Bb/E is like an E7(b5b9) voicing that omits the 3rd.

Eb/A

The same process has been used to create the second chord in this sequence.

Eb/A = A7(b5b9) with the 3rd omitted

E/D

In bar three, superimposing an E Major triad over a D bass note results in a chord that can be interpreted as Dmaj7#11. It shares the major tonality of our original Dmaj7 chord, but has the characteristic unresolved, spacious Lydian sound to it. This chord opens up the possibility of many different approaches one could take when improvising over it.

F/B

In bar four, we revert to the original idea of implying a 7(b5b9) tonality. F/B = B7(b5b9) with the 3rd omitted.

Two-Beat Feel Examples

Example 15a

Example 15b

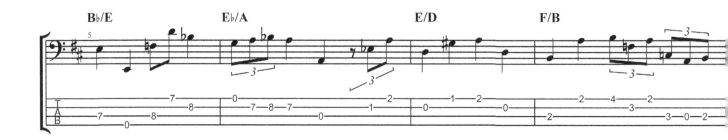

Example 15c

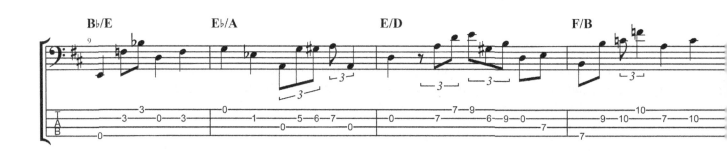

Example 15d

Here are the final set of walking examples.

Walking Examples

Example 15e

Example 15f

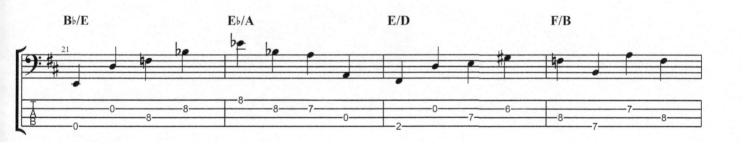

Example 15g

Example 15h

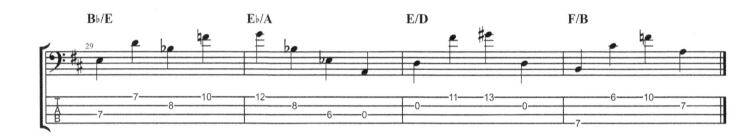

And here is the final etude.

Example 15i

Walking

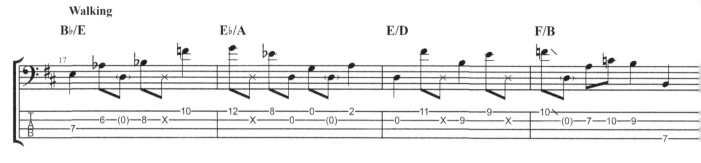

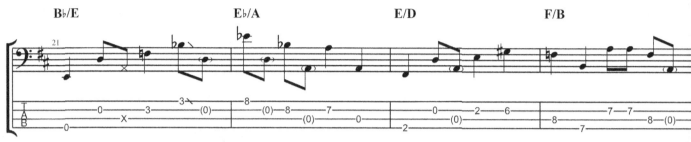

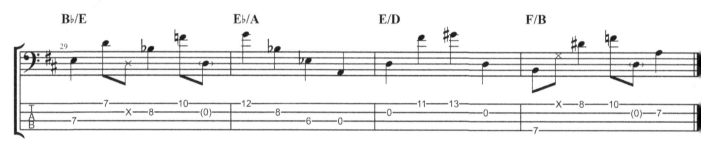

Conclusion

The purpose of this book has been twofold: first, to pass on my approach to composing well-conceived melodic basslines over common jazz progressions, illustrated in the etudes you've learnt, and second to reinforce the importance of *groove*.

By working on your two-beat feel, I hope you've arrived at a deeper understanding of time and groove. Time and groove are the mode of transmission of all harmony. It's possible to have a deep theoretical knowledge of music, to know all the notes in every position on the fretboard/fretboard, even to be able to articulate advanced ideas, and yet still sound robotic because time and groove are lacking. All the things that people think are so hip in jazz are communicated primarily via rhythm – because rhythm is the backbone.

Going forward, listen to as much music as you can by the acoustic jazz bass masters – especially Ray Brown and Ron Carter. Listen to how they create interest, movement and a deep sense of swing by varying the length of notes, playing ghost notes, and articulating phrases with hammer-ons and pull-offs. These articulations are what makes a bassline *live*.

A useful exercise is to pick one of your favorite standard tunes and to listen to multiple versions. For each version, check out what the bass player made of the tune. How did they approach it and where did they take the music? How did they navigate the harmony? What did they do to create momentum or pull back the feel? Set about transcribing your favorite version of the tune.

Above all, have fun and never stop learning. Playing the bass, especially jazz bass, is a lifetime's work. Learn and draw inspiration from as many different sources as you can.

John Patitucci

Made in the USA
Las Vegas, NV
02 January 2024

83768030R00057